To Speak or Not to Speak...

...in Tongues, That Is

O.W. McInnis

PriorityONE
publications
Detroit, MI USA

PriorityONE Publications
P. O. Box 34722 / Detroit, MI 48234
E-mail: info@priorityonebooks.com
URL: http://www.priorityonebooks.com
1 (313) 312-5318

ISBN 13:   978-1-933972-45-9
ISBN 10:   1-933972-45-9

Illustrations by Jeffery A. Brown
Cover & Interior design by Christina Dixon

Printed in the United States of America

This book is dedicated to

Julia

The wife that I needed
when I needed her the most.

Acknowledgements

Folklore, my personal library and the histories of churches from diverse cultures played an important role in the research and development of this book. However, certain individuals are to be commended for the invaluable assistance and contribution that they made towards the final product. First, I want to thank Ms. Celestine DeLoatch and Dr. James Satterfield for making accessible to me materials from the voluminous collections of the Norfolk State University Library. I would also like to recognize and thank artist, Jeffery A. Brown for his illustrations; Oretha for her typesetting and technical assistance; Evelyn, Genevieve, Shirlee and Ralston for being there; Hill's Printing Company for *(original)* publication.

~ * ~

It is with great love and respect that the children of the author posthumously release the second edition of this book through PriorityONE Publications.

Acknowledgments

Contents

Contents

Introduction

This writing is the outgrowth of much prayer and long periods of thought, study, meditation, observation and association.

The purpose of this book is, in a small measure, to shed some light on a very controversial doctrinal issue apparent within the Christian church today. The effects of this issue can be noticed in most, if not all, Christian denominations in America; and have been responsible for divisions of families, friends and Christian fellowships on many social and religious levels. Namely, that of which I speak is the issue of *"glossolalia"* or speaking in tongues as the evidence of the baptism, or the filling, of the Holy Ghost.

This book is by no means designed to reconvert those spirit-filled Christians who have had the experience of reaching an emotional summit in prayers or praises or meditations by which they were ushered into a religious orbit that caused them, for a brief moment, to make ecstatic utterances in a language unknown to others or themselves. But rather the book is meant to enlighten and encourage those spirit-filled Christians who have not been so emotionally enraptured in their Christian experiences, many of whom could not have reached such an emotional summit had they endeavored to do so.

These Christians are often made to feel by those who have had the experience of speaking in tongues that either they have been denied the most valuable gift in their search for spiritual fulfillment or that they are in a church or denomination that is unable to help them attain such a high spiritual level. Some are even made to feel that they have never been born again.

After having read this book, it is the author's prayer that all Christians will be satisfied with and use, to the best of their ability, whatever gift, *charisma,* God has given them and seek only for more of what they already have. The scripture says, *"He giveth more grace"* (James 4:6). St. Paul also instructs the Corinthian Christians that the Spirit divides the gifts *"to every man severally as He will"* (I Cor. 12:11).

The following exhortation of Paul to the Romans is applicable to all gifts of grace obtained only through faith by all Christians:

> *"...as your spiritual teacher I give this piece of advice to each one of you. Don't cherish exaggerated ideas of yourself or your importance, but try to have a sane estimate of your capabilities by the light of faith that God has given to you all. For just as you have many members in one physical body and those members differ in their function, so we, though many in number, compose one body in Christ and all are members of one another. Through the grace of God we have different gifts. If our gift is preaching, let us preach to the limit of our vision. If it is serving others, let us concentrate on our service; if it is teaching, let us give all that we have to our teaching; and if our gift be the stimulating of the faith of others, let us set ourselves to it. Let the man who is called to give, give freely; let the man who wields authority, think of his responsibility; and let the man who feels sympathy for his fellows act cheerfully."*

(Romans 12:3 – 8, Phillips – The New Testament in Modern English)

Though the gifts of grace cited by Paul in Romans 12:3–8, I Corinthians 12: 4–14, and Ephesians 4:7–14 are not all the same in number and name, yet in each the apostle endeavors to show that the diversities of the gifts of grace are necessary to form one body in Christ. Then, how is it that most of those who speak in unknown tongues have given tongues such exaggerated and unscriptural priority over all other gifts of the Spirit and contend that **all** must speak in tongues at least once, as an evidence of having been filled with the Holy Ghost? Why is it that no other gift is granted by them such approbation even though tongues is one of the least significant of gifts, as mentioned in I Corinthians 12:7–11?

This book is intended, if possible, to shed some light on these and like discrepancies regarding speaking in tongues or ecstatic utterance.

CONTROVERSY OF

THE TONGUE ISSUE

~ CHAPTER I ~
Controversy of the Tongue Issue

Only until speaking in tongues was prioritized by the Pentecostal movements at the turn of the century was it ever so great a controversial issue in the Christian church.

From the second century until the new awakening of tongues in the late 19th and early 20th centuries, speaking in tongues was never considered by the church to be the categorical evidence of the gift of the Holy Ghost, that is, all other gifts of the Spirit were presumed to come with the gift of tongues.

There was, seemingly during the latter part of the nineteenth century, a quest for rediscovery of the Spirit of God that led to the Wesleyan evangelical revivals. It was during that short period of time that many of the presently existing holiness denominations were founded. They were established by men and groups who, without any knowledge of one another, were in search of a deeper and fuller spiritual experience in their Christian lives. The denominations to which they belonged were not helping them to attain this experience; in fact, they seemed opposed to it.

Many of them were not desirous to start other denominations but, because of their zeal for Christ and His Word, some were cast out of the mainline denominations as heretics, religious fanatics or crazy "man" as Festus referred to the apostle Paul (cf. Acts 26:24, 25). Others were forced to leave their denominations because of severe and unbearable persecutions and abuses. But all, having had an experience of the sanctifying power of the Holy Ghost, were desirous and determined to show that all who would have the same experience could have it. They dared not compromise. As one who was put out of his denomination summed it up in the chorus of one of his hymns:

> *"I will not yield, I will be free.*
> *Sin shall no more reign over me.*
> *God will sufficient grace supply.*

Before I'll yield I'll die."
Charles Price Jones

Though written and set to music by one person, it was the sentiment of all those who had suffered like reproaches.

As has been said, these "religious rejects" were not interested in starting new denominations. Being scattered throughout the United States without any former knowledge of one another, they did not organize themselves; they mostly called themselves holiness movements; and if allowed, they served in any denomination. They endeavored to be non-sectarian and non-denominational. The motto of one group was "Denominationalism is slavery."[1] Their chief endeavor was holiness of life. They strongly espoused the Wesleyan doctrine of entire sanctification; having tasted and seen that the Lord is good (cf. Psalm 34:8).

"But alas! The sectarian spirit is hard to conquer. We are soon contending for our own crown, our

---

[1] *Manual of the History, Doctrine, Government and Ritual of the Church of Christ (Holiness) U.S.A.,* Rev. Ed., 1986, p. 12.

doctrine, our way, our sect instead of the Lord. Please read I Corinthians 1, 2, and 3."[2] At the turn of the century those fragmentary groups began to organize into denominations under different names in different locations.

In the spring of 1906, the news was heralded throughout the country that a revival was being conducted by Rev. William J. Seymour at the Azusa Street Mission in Los Angeles, California; a revival of which many believed that the events that transpired on the day of Pentecost were being experienced anew. Many, it was said, were receiving the baptism of the Holy Ghost evidenced by speaking in tongues. At hearing this, representatives from many of the newly formed holiness movements went to Los Angeles to investigate the mystery. Many of those who went to see what it was all about began either to speak in tongues or believed that they were witnessing the return of Pentecost as recorded in Acts 2:4. The following somewhat became the testimony of many members of Pentecostal movements: "I'm saved and sanctified; baptized with the Holy Ghost and that with fire, speaking

[2] Ibid., p. 12.

in tongues as the Spirit gives utterance according to Acts 2:4."

But not all leaders of holiness movements accepted speaking in tongues as the definitive evidence of the baptism of the Holy Ghost. There were some who believed speaking in tongues ceased after the apostolic age. Others contended that speaking in tongues is not the primary evidence of the baptism or filling of the Holy Ghost. Still, others looked upon it as a passing fancy that soon would cease ticking, like a spring driven clock, for lack of something to impel it. How wrong they were! Some even conceived in their minds that speaking in tongues in worship services was satanically induced. So as the doctrine of speaking in tongues in the church spread throughout all holiness factions, the opposition to that belief spread likewise, creating divisions among some of the newly formed organizations, and thus separating families, friends and fellowships.

Though practically all holiness movements and Pentecostal movements still believe in sanctification as a work of grace subsequent to justification, all believe in holiness of life in this present world, and all refer primarily to the same scriptures to substantiate their beliefs, the controversy of tongues still remains among them. Each faction is still relentlessly holding onto and strongly fostering their beliefs and interpretations on the issue.

Though many Pentecostal denominations differ on marginal issues in doctrines, they all espouse the doctrine of speaking in tongues as the evidence of the baptism or filling of the Holy Ghost. They all contend that those who have never spoken in tongues have never experienced or received the baptism of the Holy Ghost. In spite of visible signs of other gifts of grace in non-tongue speaking believers, the general contention of Pentecostals is that one must speak in tongues at least once as the evidence of having experienced the baptism of the Holy Ghost. This is a statement that one would have to read between the lines of scripture to find, or erroneously weave into the scripture.

Recently, a famous television evangelist emphatically declared that no person can do

God's work successfully unless he has been baptized with the Holy Ghost and speaks in tongues. Yet this evangelist believes in and espouses John Wesley's doctrine of entire sanctification. Notwithstanding their declarations, John Wesley, one of the most successful evangelists in the history of Christianity, never spoke in tongues. Time and space will not permit me to mention the names and works of others whose labors helped spread the Christian faith long before the surge of modern Pentecostalism to regions where the name of Jesus had never been known.

While non-Pentecostals do not deny that unknown tongues were spoken in the Corinthian church as mentioned in the 12th, 13th, and 14th chapters of I Corinthians, they do contend that if one speaks in an unknown tongue, it should be done according to I Corinthians 14:27-32 where Paul gives definite guidelines for the use of ethnic or unknown tongues in public worship services. In the event that one does speak in an unknown tongue (contrary to the general Pentecostal practice where many who are so emotionally overcome do start speaking in tongues) Paul instructs ". . . let it be by two or at the most three." And instead of the two or three speaking all at once, to avoid confusion, Paul says, "And that by course," or in turns, or one after the other. "And let one interpret," Paul continues. "But if there be no interpreter, let him (the speaker) be silent in the church; and let him speak to himself and to God. Let the prophets (the ones to whom God has revealed his purpose) speak two or three (one at a time) and let the others judge." i.e., think carefully and discern what was said.

If one sitting in the congregation receives a revelation, Paul says, "let the first (the main speaker) hold his peace." This practice of courtesy is followed in most evangelical churches in Bible lessons, seminars and Sunday Schools.

In order for all to edify and comfort one another, Paul allowed as many as desired to speak, but only "one by one, that all may learn and be comforted." To accomplish this, Paul seems to say, whether one speaks in his own language or ecstatic utterance, one should be clearly understood or else the meeting will result only in confusion.

Some Pentecostals contend that when the Holy Ghost strikes, one has to speak in tongues in obedience to the Spirit. This by no means coincides with the teaching of the Apostle Paul in I Corinthians 14:32, "The spirits (gifts for service) of the prophets are subject to the prophets." Note that the gift is subject to and not superior to the prophet. That means the prophet, not the gift, is in "the driver's seat," i.e., in control. So if anyone in a service is moved by a spirit he or she cannot control, be well assured that it is not the Holy Ghost. The Holy Ghost is not an instigator of confusion. "For God is not the author of confusion but of peace, as in all the churches of the saints" (I Cor. 14:33).

St. Paul ends I Corinthians, Chapters 12 and 14, on the same high note. In I Corinthians 12:31 he says, "But covet earnestly the best gifts." He implies that the best gifts are those gifts that best serve the church. He further specifies that one of the best gifts is the gift of prophesy, which is second only to apostleship as cited in I

Corinthians 12:28. He also says, "Wherefore, brethren, covet to prophesy, and forbid not to speak with tongues. Let all things be done decently and in order" (I Cor. 14:39, 40).

As for evidence, the manifestation of truth there is nowhere found in the Holy Scriptures that speaking in tongues is the specific sign or evidence of the baptism of the Holy Ghost. In fact, the scriptures do not ascribe as categorical evidence any gift or gifts of the Spirit as cited by Paul in I Corinthians 12:28; Romans 12:5-9; Ephesians 4:11, 12. Only the gift of love, which is "shed abroad in our hearts by the Holy Ghost," can be called the categorical evidence of the presence of the Holy Ghost (Rom. 5:5b). In St. John 13:35 Jesus declared, "By this shall all men know that ye are my disciples if ye have love one to another." St. John, in his epistle, writes, "Beloved, if God so loved us, we ought also to love one another. No man hath seen God at any time. If we love one another, God dwelleth in us, and his love is perfected in us. Hereby know we that we dwell in him, and he in us, because he hath given us of his Spirit" (I John 4:11-13).

In the thirteenth chapter of I Corinthians, Paul places love above all other spiritual gifts, even prophecy, as the unmistakable and ever-abiding manifestation of the Spirit-filled life. This is the one gift that all Christians should pursue, possess and practice.

The gifts cited by Paul in I Corinthians 13:1-3 – tongues, prophecy, understanding of mysteries, knowledge, faith, benevolence and sacrificial death – were being practiced or simulated by non-Christians; i.e., heathens. Charity, divine love, can neither be satanically influenced nor imitated. So if tongues, the gift most highly esteemed by the Corinthians and given priority over other gifts by most Pentecostals, can be and is being simulated by Satan, then Christianity is left without a lasting foundation to prove its credibility. For, "Whether there be tongues, they shall cease" (cf. I Corinthians 13:8).

Therefore Paul exhorts Christians to "follow after charity, and desire (not follow after) spiritual gifts, but rather that ye prophesy" (I Corinthians 14:1).

Therefore if one has unconditionally committed one's life to Christ in love and obedience with willingness to serve, leave the distribution of the spiritual gifts to the Holy Spirit who knows exactly what gift or gifts one is most capable and qualified to use for service in the church. But follow, chase, pursue after charity. Let charity be the cardinal object of your quest.

TONGUES
BEFORE
PENTECOST

~ CHAPTER II ~
Tongues before Pentecost

Though Pentecost signaled the rising of a new and different religion on the horizon of time, it was accompanied by phenomena not altogether unlike those that had been witnessed in some other religious settings among the more ancient and primitive people; e.g., shouting and praising and speaking in tongues. This will be dealt with more distinctly in a later chapter.

There were instances of speaking in tongues or ecstatic utterances many centuries before Christ. Biblical and non-Biblical histories explicitly record examples of trances, séances, enchantments, fainting, incantations and other paroxysms, characterized by uncontrollable passions, actions and utterances, all under the guise of some form of religion. However, this does not indicate that all phenomenal experiences were satanically influenced. Yet it should be a reminder that whether stimuli are divinely,

31

satanically, or merely emotionally induced, they can and may produce similar responses which can be misleading unless the person or persons who experience or witness them are able to perceive the differences. It should also be a reminder that whatever part *feeling* may play in one's religion, *feeling* should never be the deciding factor in determining whether a stimulus is from God or Satan. "...but the just shall live by his faith," not by his *feeling* (Hab. 2:4b, Rom. 1:17b).

Some of the earliest Biblical examples of ecstatic utterances and behavior preceding Pentecost are recorded in the Old Testament.

First, according to Numbers 11:25-29, God took of the spirit that was on Moses and gave it to the seventy chosen men of the elders of Israel. "When the spirit rested on them, they prophesied; but they did not do so again" (Num. 11:24b, NIV).

There were two other men of the seventy, Eldad and Medad, who remained in the camp. "Yet the spirit of the Lord also rested on them and they prophesied in the camp" (Num. 11:26, NIV).

The word "prophesy" here does not refer to foretelling the future, but rather, a gushing forth of praising and glorifying God. "It had reference to a certain frenzy or emotional excitement which was considered a manifestation of the Spirit of God."[3]

No doubt they were all so emotionally overcome with joy they went into ecstatic frenzies and words poured forth in praise either in an unknown tongue or words in their native tongue without cognition, not previously meditated on.

This phenomenon evidently ceased after that occasion since no such example was ever mentioned in the scripture during the ministry of the seventy elders. But this, by no means, denies that this was the work of the Spirit of God.

A second example of ecstatic utterance and behavior was demonstrated when Israel was camped in the Plains of Moab as told in Numbers 22 – 24. King Balak of Moab, for fear of Israel,

[3] The Book of Numbers, *The Interpreters Bible,* Vol. II, 1953, Abingdon Press, New York, p. 198.

sent for Balaam to come and curse Israel for him. Balaam was a soothsayer who evidently had some prophetic gift and could be used of God; not because God condoned soothsaying, but only on this occasion to frustrate the purpose of Balak against Israel.

Balak had Balaam to view Israel from several different places (cf. Num. 22:41; 23:13, 27). Balaam sought enchantments, i.e., some natural or mystical means by which soothsayers were sometimes able to predict future events. But in each case, God, in His sovereign will, interrupted and gave a word to Balaam to speak to Balak. Twice Balaam confessed he received his message while in a trance – an unconscious state in which one's ability to function voluntarily is suspended. Though no reference is given of speaking in an unknown tongue, it is quite obvious that Balaam's unusual utterances and actions took place while in such a state of ecstasy.

A third example is seen when Saul was chosen to be the first king of Israel. Saul was instructed by Samuel that he would meet a company of prophets, "And the Spirit of the Lord will come upon thee, and thou shalt prophesy with them" (I Sam. 10:6). As Samuel promised, Saul met the company of prophets and the Spirit of God came upon him, and he prophesied among them" (I Sam. 10:10). That is, he fell into an abnormal psychic state which expressed itself in song and prophetic ecstasy, not foretelling, but an unusual gushing forth of praise with an abundance of unintelligible words with little or no otherwise significance.

Still a fourth example of unconventional utterance and behavior recorded in scripture also concerns Saul who sent messengers to seek and apprehend David in Naioth of Ramah. "And when they saw the company of prophets prophesying and Samuel standing as appointed over them, the Spirit of God was upon the messengers of Saul and they prophesied. And when it was told Saul, he sent other messengers and they prophesied likewise. And Saul sent messengers again the third time, and they prophesied also" (I Sam. 19:20-21).

Saul's only intent was to find David and kill him. So he went also to Ramah. On his way, the Spirit of God came upon him and he prophesied all the way from Sechu to Naioth in Ramah. When he saw Samuel, he prophesied and stripped off his clothes and lay down naked all day and all night (cf. I Sam. 19:22-24).

No other episode in scripture lends itself better to the explanation of ecstatic utterance and behavior than the episode of Saul (cf. I Sam. 10:1-7; 19:18-24).

It almost seems unthinkable that the Spirit of God would come upon Saul while he searched for David to kill him. Maybe this verse of an 18th century hymn can shed some light on it:

> *Deep in unfathomable mines,*
> *Of never failing skill*
> *He treasures up His bright designs,*
> *And works His sovereign will."*

William Cowper

A final and fifth occasion of ecstatic utterance and behavior is found in I Kings 18:17-29. A description of the eight hundred prophets of Baal is presented in the narrative of Elijah's encounter with Ahab and all Israel on Mount Carmel.

Elijah, Ahab and all Israel stood by and watched as the prophets of Baal called on Baal "from morning until noon. And they leaped upon the altar" (v. 26). "They cried aloud and cut themselves after their manner with knives and lancets, till blood gushed out upon them" (v. 28).

Here again can be clearly seen evidence of ecstatic utterances and behavior as these prophets of Baal worked themselves into a frenzy which expressed itself in "endless repeated shrieks and cries. . . Such actions frequently led to a state of rapture that resembled madness or they cut themselves or one another with knives and lances till their bodies were covered with blood or they fell into a swoon."[4]

In contrast Elijah quietly rebuilt the altar of the Lord with twelve stones, cut the bullock in pieces

---

[4] Hartman, Louis F., *The Encyclopedic Dictionary of the Bible,* McGraw-Hill Book Company, Inc., New York, 1963. (Columns 1932-1933)

on the altar and called upon the God of Abraham, Isaac and Jacob.

While occasional references may be found in the Old Testament where the Spirit's presence is accompanied by some vocal outburst, in the majority of the examples where the Spirit of God is active, there is no reference to speaking or ecstatic utterances.[5]

This was true in the case of Elijah. Elijah never went into a frenzy nor lost self-control or his sense of reason. Yet it is quite evident that the Spirit of God was upon him.

Elijah made a quiet and simple appeal to God saying, "Lord God of Abraham, Isaac and of Israel, let it be known this day that thou art God in Israel , and that I am your servant, and that I have done all these things at thy word. Hear me, O Lord, hear me, that this people may know that thou art the Lord God and thou hast turned their hearts back again. Then the fire of the Lord fell" (I Kings 18:36-38).

---

[5] Donald S. Metz, *Speaking in Tongues,* Nazarene Publishing Co., Kansas City, Kansas, p. 21.

However, *"glossolalia"* – speaking in tongues – was never restricted to the Judaeo-Christian experience. Similar phenomena of unknown tongues have been observed in primitive cultures throughout history.

Will Durant, in reference to Religion in Egypt, does not mention ecstatic utterance, per se, when he tells of the Egyptian priests, "selling charms and mumbling incantations."[6]

To mumble is to speak indistinctly or utter without the use of normal words. Incantations are formulaic words or sounds used to produce a magic affect.

Durant further states that, "At every step, the pious Egyptian had to mutter strange formulas to avert evil and attract good."[7]

---

[6] Will Durant, *Our Oriental Heritage,* Simon and Schuster, New York, p. 204.
[7] Ibid.

Another ancient record of ecstatic speech is contained in the "Report of Wenamun," written about 1100 B.C.

Wenamun, an Egyptian envoy sent by Herihor the High Priest of Amun to Byblos to procure cedar from the Lebanon forest to build a sacred barge for Amun, was not received by Zakar-Baal, the Prince of Byblos. After nineteen days a young attendant to the Prince fell into a prophetic frenzy and demanded of Zakar-Baal that Wenamun be received and treated honorably.

The report said, "Now, when he sacrificed to his god, the god seized one of his noble youth, making him frenzy, so that he (Zakar-Baal) said, "Bring him (Wenamon) hither."[8] The young unnamed prophet was so possessed that he continued in a prophetic frenzy during the night. Wenamon continues, "Now while the youth continued in frenzy, I found a ship to Egypt and I loaded all my belongings into it."[9]

---

[8] Breasted, James Henry, *Ancient Records of Egypt,* The University of Chicago Press, Chicago, 1905, Vol. IV, p. 280.
[9] Ibid.

This young prophet is described as god-possessed. His ecstatic speech is considered as inspired by God. He is a dedicated worshipper of Amon, a pagan god referred to as No in Jeremiah 46:25.

In the Dialogues of Plato (429-347 B.C.), it is by no means difficult to conclude that ecstatic utterance appeared in Greece at least four centuries before Christ.

In the Dialogues, ecstatic speech is referred to by Socrates. In the Timaeus, Socrates says, "No man, when in his wits, attains prophetic truth and inspiration."[10] But he receives it when "his intelligence is enthralled in sleep or, he is demented (crazed) by some distemper or possession."[11] While in this state the man sees visions and utters words that he cannot understand. "But while he continues demented, he cannot judge the vision which he sees or the words which he utters."[12] Under such circumstances, "it is customary to appoint interpreters to be judges of the true

---

[10] *Dialogue of Plato,* Benjamin Jowett, trans., Random House Inc., New York, 1937, Vol. I, p.50
[11] Ibid.
[12] Ibid.

inspiration."[13] They are, "expositors of dark sayings and visions."[14]

In the *Phaedrus,* Socrates said, "There is a madness which is a divine gift, and the source of the chiefest blessings granted to men."[15]

Socrates continues, "Madness is superior to a sound mind, for the one is only human but the other of divine origin."[16]

And where plagues and woes are bred in certain families because of some ancient blood guiltiness, "There madness has entered with holy prayers and rites and by inspired utterance found a way of deliverance."[17]

Another kind of madness alluded to by Socrates is the "madness of those who are possessed by the Muses; which taking hold of a delicate and virgin soul, and there inspiring frenzy, awakens lyrics

---

[13] Ibid.
[14] Ibid.
[15] Ibid., p. 248
[16] Ibid., p. 249
[17] Ibid.

and all other numbers."[18] Socrates refers to ecstasy as madness from a divine source.

An example of ecstatic utterance in Rome appears in the sixth book of the Aeneid by Virgil (70-19 B.C.)

In this episode, Aeneas, seeking divine guidance, "seeks the fortress where Apollo set high enthroned, and the lone mystery of the awful Sibyl's cavern depth, over whose mind and soul the prophetic Delian breathes high inspiration and reveals futurity."[19]

As Sibyl, the Priestess speaks from a cavern cut in the side of the Euboic cliff, "Her wild heart heaves madly in her panting bosom... and her voice is more than mortal, now that the gods breathe on her."[20]

When completely possessed by the god Apollo, the Sibyl "chants from the shrine her perplexing

---

[18] Ibid.

[19] Virgil, *The Aeneid,* trans. J. W. Mackail, The Modern Library, New York, 1950, p. 104.

[20] Ibid., p. 105

terror, echoing through the cavern truth wrapped in obscurity."[21]

No doubt, speaking in tongues was accepted as part of the religious worship of the ancient peoples, except the Israelites, before the coming of Christ.

What better proof would one need that speaking in tongues appeared in Greece before Christ and outside the Christian church than I Corinthians 12:1-3? Even though Paul's letter to the Corinthian church was written about 57 A.D., he prefaced his discourse on spiritual gifts stating, "Now concerning spiritual gifts, brethren, I would not have you ignorant. Ye know that ye were Gentiles, carried away unto these dumb idols, even as ye were led. Wherefore I give you to understand, that no man speaking by the Spirit of God calleth Jesus accursed; and that no man can say that Jesus is the Lord but by the Holy Ghost."

Now the evidence that Paul was referring to the gifts of tongues in his preface is unquestionable in

---

[21] Ibid., p. 106

that he placed special emphasis on that gift throughout the three chapters. In I Corinthians 12:1, Paul assured the Corinthian Christians of his desire to fully enlighten them on the subject of spiritual gifts. In the second verse, he reminded them that prior to their conversion to the Christian faith they were heathens, worshippers of dumb idols, having been led by skillful prophets and prophetesses of idol gods. As heathens, the Corinthians were well acquainted with the emotionalism associated with ancient pagan worship.

Adam Clark presents the following viewpoint as it pertains to verse 2 of I Corinthians 12, "...hurried by your passions into a senseless worship, the chief part of which was calculated only to excite and gratify animal propensities."[22]

Paul proceeds in verse 3 to assist them in the discrimination of tongues. Having been exposed to religions of the eastern cults, the new converts had witnessed, maybe even experienced, the impassioned impulses which led to glossolalia.

---

[22] Adam Clark, *Clark's Commentary,* Vol. 4, Abingdon Press, New York, p. 257.

Paul gives them a standard by which they could discern the differences between tongues inspired by satanic forces and tongues inspired by the gift of God. *"No man speaking by the Spirit of God calleth Jesus accursed."*

It would seem that if speaking in tongues were the categorical evidence of the indwelling of the Holy Ghost, the instructions contained in verse 3 would be unnecessary to the Corinthian converts. However, Paul is saying that through ecstatic utterance it was possible, whether knowingly or unknowingly, to call Jesus accursed by either denying his sonship or honoring someone or something as equal to or superior to him.

"And that no man can say that Jesus is the Lord but by the Holy Ghost." The same Spirit that restrained from calling Jesus accursed gives strong inspiration for calling Jesus the Lord, not by mere utterance of words but by the experience of the indwelling persuasion of the Holy Ghost (please read Matt. 16:17 and I John 4:1-3).

TONGUES DURING THE APOSTOLIC PERIOD

PETER AT THE HOUSE OF CORNELIUS

~ CHAPTER III ~
Tongues During the Apostolic Period

"And it shall come to pass afterward that I will pour out my spirit upon all flesh; and your sons and your daughters shall prophesy, your old men shall dream dreams, your young men shall see visions: And also upon the servants and upon the handmaids in those days will I pour out my spirit" (Joel 2:28, 29).

"I indeed baptize you with water unto repentance: but he that cometh after me is mightier than I, whose shoes I am not worthy to bear: he shall baptize you with the Holy Ghost and with fire" (Matt. 3:11).

"And he (Jesus) said unto them, go ye into all the world and preach the gospel to every creature. He that believeth and is baptized shall be saved: but he that believeth not shall be damned. And these signs shall follow them that believe; In my name shall they cast out devils; they shall speak with new tongues; They shall take up serpents; and if they drink any deadly thing, it shall not hurt them; they shall lay hands on the sick, and they shall recover (Mark 16:15-18).

"But ye shall receive power after that the Holy Ghost is come upon you: and ye shall be witnesses unto me both in Jerusalem and in Judaea and in Samaria and unto the uttermost part of the earth" (Acts 1:8).

These four passages of scripture point directly to the day of Pentecost. In the Old Testament, Pentecost, the second of three annual pilgrimage feasts, was the time that all Israel, especially men, had to visit the house of the Lord (cf. Ex. 34:23; Deut. 16:16). In Exodus 23:16, it is called "the feast of harvest... and feast of ingathering"; in Exodus 34:22, "the feast of weeks, of the first fruits of wheat." In Numbers 28:26, "the day of first fruits." And in Deuteronomy 16:10, "the feast of weeks." It was referred to as "the feast of weeks" because it was celebrated seven weeks and one day after the Passover (cf. Lev. 23:15, 16; Deut. 16:9)

The word *Pentecost* is translated from the Greek, *"pentekoste,"* meaning fiftieth day. The fiftieth day after Passover was a day of great rejoicing and thanksgiving because it came on the day when the Jews offered to God the first fruits of the wheat harvest. It was at this particular feast that

God designed the inauguration of a new religion; new, not only in time, but new in origin, new in quality, new in purpose and new in destiny. So significant is this day on the Christian calendar that it is still traditionally observed in mainline churches.

St. Luke, in his writing of the Acts of the Apostles, dramatically reveals the events of the first Pentecost as it occurred after the crucifixion, resurrection and ascension. Luke writes that at this time, *"... there were dwelling at Jerusalem Jews, devout men, out of every nation under heaven"* (Acts 2:5). There were also in attendance at the feast Jews of the dispersion with Gentiles, strangers of Rome and proselytes, i.e., persons from throughout the Roman Empire beyond the region of Judaea (cf. Acts 2:9-11).

Possibly there were representatives of every language and dialect and culture of the known world who witnessed the phenomenon of the descent of the Holy Ghost upon the one hundred and twenty ardent believers and followers of Jesus. This, no doubt, was the initial fulfillment of the words of Jesus to his disciples as recorded in Acts 1:8b, *"and ye shall be witnesses unto me both in Jerusalem, and in all Judaea and in Samaria, and unto the uttermost part of the earth."*

On the day of his ascension, ten days before Pentecost, Jesus *"being assembled together with them* (His disciples) *commanded them that they should not depart from Jerusalem, but wait for the promise of the Father, which, saith he, ye have heard of me. For John truly baptized with water; but ye shall be baptized with the Holy Ghost not many days hence"* (Acts 1:4, 5; Luke 24:49).

In obedience to the command of Jesus, the disciples tarried – waited -- in Jerusalem, very likely in fervent prayer and with eager expectation for the fulfillment *"of the promise of the Father,"* not knowing in what fashion it would come (Acts 1:4).

"And when the day of Pentecost was fully come, they were all with one accord in one place. And suddenly there came a sound from heaven as of a rushing mighty wind, and it filled all the house where they were sitting. And there appeared unto them cloven tongues like as of fire, and it sat upon each of them. And they were all filled with the Holy Ghost, and began to speak with other tongues as the Spirit gave them utterance" (Acts 2:1-4).

Upon the filling of the Holy Ghost the one hundred twenty *"began to speak with other (heterais) tongues (glossais)."* Not unknown tongues as spoken in the Corinthian Church, but **other** ethnic dialects *(dialekto)* which were equally intelligible to all races and nationalities which were present at the feast. This was the fulfillment of the words of Jesus to his disciples in St. Mark 16:17 when he said, *"...they shall speak with new (kainais) tongues."* This meant qualitatively new, as contrasted with chronologically new *(Neos)* or new in time.

The tongues spoken on the Day of Pentecost by the disciples required no interpreter. Immediately upon the disciples' utterance, the multitude heard and understood in their particular dialects, e.g., the different languages commonly spoken in the provinces from which they came.

Consider verse 6 of Acts, Chapter 2 which states, *"Now when this was noised abroad, the multitude came together."* Some commentators believe that it was the noise of the *"rushing mighty wind"* (v. 2) heard by the multitude. But there seems not to be the slightest indication in scripture that the multitude heard the wind nor saw the fiery tongues. Both phenomena occurred in "the house where they were sitting" (v. 2b). This miracle, no doubt, was given only to those who waited for the *"promise of the Father."*

Upon hearing the disciples speak in tongues, the multitude was confounded. Were they confounded because they heard them speaking in tongues? Not by any means. Throughout the Roman Empire, speaking in tongues played an important part in pagan religions. This was common knowledge to some, or maybe most, of the multitude present. Though speaking in tongues was never a part of religious worship among the Jews, "tongues" was not the reason for their being confounded and amazed. Knowing that all those that spoke in tongues were Galileans who probably spoke in the Aramaic tongue, the popular language of Palestine at that time, the multitude *"was confounded because that every man heard them speak in his own (dialekto) language. And, they were all amazed and marveled, saying one to another, Behold, are not all these which speak Galilaeans? And how hear we every man in our own tongue, wherein we were born?"* (Acts 2:6-8)

So the multitude was not confounded and amazed because of the speaking in tongues, but because every man heard and understood in his own language, without an interpreter. On the other hand, the pagan prophets and prophetesses, who, when possessed by the gods, in a state of ecstasy saw visions and uttered strange sayings. However, this phenomenon required "expositors of dark sayings and visions" to interpret what was said and what the visions meant.[23]

Neither did the disciples ever lose control of their behavior or sense of reason. As the multitude looked on, they observed among the disciples an ecstatic, yet sane, pouring forth in their (multitude) tongues, *the wonderful works of God. And they were all amazed and were in doubt, saying one to another, 'What meaneth this?'"* (Acts 2:11, 12). They were amazed to see such sanity prevailing in a company of religious worshippers; something that was not common in pagan worship where trances, fainting, ecstatic utterances and frenzied behavior prevailed.

---

[23] Jowett, loc. Cit., Vol. I, p. 50.

Some mysteries of Pentecost will ever remain mysteries.

First, the scripture does not specify what languages were spoken by the disciples on the Day of Pentecost. Jesus simply said, *"They shall speak with new tongues"* (Mark 16:17). Luke says in Acts 2:4, *"They began to speak with other tongues."* Neither used the phrase, "unknown tongues."

Second, the scripture does not say whether the disciples even knew what tongues they spoke in themselves. They spoke *"as the Spirit gave them utterance"* (Acts 2:4b).

In an attempt to explain the mystery, one commentator has said, "In these moments of ecstasy, the disciples, possessed by the Spirit, uttered sounds inarticulate and incoherent, which the hearers fancied were words of a strange language, and in their simplicity tried to interpret. They listened eagerly to the medley of sounds and explained them by their own extemporaneous thoughts. Each of them had recourse to his own native patois (regional dialect) to supply some meaning to the unintelligible accent, and generally succeeded in affixing to them the thoughts that were uppermost in his own mind."[24]

This concept practically rules out the Pentecostal miracle and its real intention. It gave the hearer the privilege to hear and translate the "unintelligible sounds by the thoughts uppermost in his own mind," – whether right or wrong.

But the miracle of Pentecost was by no means on the part of the hearers. It was all the work of the Holy Ghost working in and through the disciples. So whatever tongues in which the disciples spoke, or whether they knew what they were saying, it was the Holy Ghost that translated their utterances to the multitude so that every one heard in the language wherein he was born.

There are many other issues that remain mysterious leaving latitude for speculation because the scriptures do not speak directly to those issues. But one can be contented with this

---

[24] Very Rev. H.D.M. Spence, *Pulpit Commentary on Acts and Romans,* Wm. B. Eerdsman Publishing Co., Grand Rapids, MI., p. 49

scripture: *"The secret things belong unto the Lord our God: but those things which are revealed belong unto us and to our children forever. . ."* (Deut. 29:29).

As ever, there were those who accepted this phenomenon as nothing more than a drunken and riotous crowd, *"full of new wine* (Acts 2:13). But Peter readily informed them that the ecstatic behavior they were witnessing was not the result of new wine, but the fulfilling of *"that which was spoken of by the prophet Joel; And it shall come to pass in the last days, saith God, I will pour out of my Spirit upon all flesh: and your sons and your daughters shall prophesy, and your young men shall see visions, and your old men shall dream dreams: And on my servants and on my handmaidens I will pour out in those days of my Spirit; and they shall prophesy"* (Acts 2:16b-18).

Peter, quoting from the prophesy of Joel, certainly had in mind the Hebrew word *Naba* for prophesy which means not only to foretell the future but to cause to bubble up, to pour forth words abundantly, or to speak or sing profusely and ecstatically. This, Peter said, was the response of the disciples to the outpouring of the Spirit of God upon them as promised by God in prophesy.

It is quite evident that at that particular time the disciples did not predict or preach in tongues. They poured forth praises in tongues of the wonderful works of God (cf. Acts 2:11)

There are only two other occasions where speaking in tongues are mentioned in the Acts of the Apostles.

According to Acts 10:44-46, a Gentile gathering in the house of Cornelius of Caesarea received the baptism of the Holy Ghost and responded to the experience precisely as the disciples did on the Day of Pentecost. This astounded the Jews which came with Peter from Joppa, *"Because that on the Gentiles also was poured out the gift of the Holy Ghost. For they heard them speak with tongues, and magnify God"* (Acts 10:45, 46).

In Acts 11:15, 17, Peter clearly states to the contending brethren at Jerusalem that what the disciples experienced on the Day of Pentecost the Gentile believers experienced in Cornelius' house. He declared, *"And as I began to speak the Holy Ghost fell on them, as on us at the beginning. . . Forasmuch then as God gave them the like gift as he did unto us who believed on the Lord Jesus Christ, who was I, that I could withstand God?"*

"When they (the brethren) *heard these things, they held their peace, and glorified God saying, then hath God also to the Gentiles granted repentance unto life"* (Acts 11:18). To pour out His Spirit on all flesh, as God baptized the church with the Holy Ghost on the Day of Pentecost for the sake of the Jewish nation, he also baptized the church in Cornelius' house for the sake of the Gentiles.

The other occasion of speaking in tongues occurred in Ephesus (Acts 19:1-7). While the Apostle Paul was in Ephesus, he found certain disciples who had already received the baptism of John the Baptist unto repentance, but had not received the baptism of the Holy Ghost (cf. Luke 3:2, 3, 15, 16). When Paul asked whether they received the Holy Ghost when they believed, they answered, *"We have not so much as heard whether there be any Holy Ghost"* (Acts 19:2). Then Paul asked, *"Unto what then were ye baptized? And they said, unto John's baptism"* (Acts 19:3). Then Paul proceeded to inform them that John's baptism was only to repentance but they should *"Believe on him that should come after him* (John), *that is, on Christ Jesus. When they heard this, they were baptized in the name of the Lord Jesus. And when Paul had laid his hands upon them, the Holy Ghost came on them and they spake with tongues and prophesied"* (Acts 19:4-6).

The three phenomena of speaking in tongues as recorded in the Acts of the Apostles were all experienced by different people at different times in different places and in different settings. It was the Jews at Pentecost, the Gentiles in Cornelius' house, and the disciples of John the Baptist in Ephesus. Yet all of them responded precisely the same way at the outpouring, or filling, of the Holy Ghost. They all spoke with **other** tongues and prophesied.

St. Paul's analogy to the Corinthian church regarding baptism in the Holy Ghost could apply in this case also. *"For by one Spirit are we all baptized into one body, whether we be Jews or Gentiles, whether we be bond or free, and have been all made to drink into one spirit"* (I Cor. 12:13).

The only other event of speaking in tongues as recorded in the New Testament is found in the 12th, 13th, and 14th chapters of I Corinthians.

Among the many problems existing in the church in Corinth (problems such as divisions, brothers going to court, questions about marriage, meats offered to idols, temperance at the Lord's Supper, the Resurrection and the regulation of covering of the heads of men and women in the assemblies), there was the problem of evaluating spiritual gifts and how to execute the phenomenal gift of *glossolaly* (speaking in tongues). To this issue alone Paul devoted all of the above mentioned chapters, with the exception of verses 34-38 of the 14th chapter.

It should be clearly observed that Paul was, by no means, endeavoring to promote tongues in the Corinthian church. He was well aware that speaking in tongues was capable of being generated by demonic incantations, imposters and emotional ecstasy as well as by the true Spirit of God.

Paul also realized that there were several factors that impacted on the problems at the Corinthian church. First among these factors was the presence of pagan religions that abounded in the city of Corinth. And, no doubt, there were pagan worshipers and unbelievers who frequented the worship services of the Christian assemblies. Secondly, many of the Christian converts in the church in Corinth were still wrestling to free themselves from the moral and religious traditions and practices of paganism, one of which was speaking in tongues. Paul evidently envisioned that it would be damaging to the Corinthian Christians and to the Christian faith in general to promote tongues, i.e., ecstatic utterance. Even though ecstatic utterances could be generated by many false persuasions, Paul recognized that there was a gift of the Spirit that could be expressed in *(glossa)* a tongue that was genuine. This gift Paul sets out to identify and regulate in the Corinthian church.

In I Corinthians 12:8-10, Paul cites some of the gifts but not in orderly form. In verse 28, he cites the gifts in orderly and qualitative order, placing "diversities of tongues" last. Yet the members of the church had so highly esteemed this gift that they looked with contempt on those who did not speak in tongues.

In Paul's analogy of the human body being made up of many members, each having a different but congruent function, he likens the church to the body of Christ with the spiritual gifts as members set in order by God, each performing its particular ministry, yet working in harmony with all other members (cf. I Cor. 12:12-28). But Paul says that the body would not really be a body and could not properly function if all were one member (cf. v. 19).

After classifying the gifts in numerical order in verse 28, he asked the following questions: *"Are all apostles? are all prophets? are all teachers? are all workers of miracles? Have all the gifts of healing? do all speak with tongues? do all interpret?"* (I Cor. 12:29, 30). The conclusive answer to each of these questions is an emphatic "No."

Paul uses Chapter 14 exclusively to regulate the gift of tongues in the public assemblies. His whole thesis is that no member or members should ever speak in a tongue in the assembly without being understood, without being able to either interpret his own utterance or have someone with the gift of interpretation to reveal what was uttered. "For one who speaks in a tongue speaks to God, not to men, and in his spirit he speaks mysteries," – i.e., something hidden or not fully manifested. He edifies only himself, because no man in the assembly understands what he says (cf. I Cor. 14:2, 4). But the person who *"prophesies speaks to men* (the whole church) *to edification and exhortation and comfort"* (I Cor. 14:3, 5).

Paul exhorts them in verse 12 in their zealous quest for spiritual gifts to seek the gifts by which they may *"excel to the edifying of the church."* And if one should receive in a tongue a revelation to the edifying of the church, he should *"pray that he may interpret"* (v. 13). Otherwise, however edifying the revelation may be, it would be unprofitable to the church, seeing no one knows what was said in the tongue.

Paul continues by saying, in essence, that *"glossalalia,"* speaking in tongues, may take the form of praying, singing, bestowing blessings and giving of thanks or praising. If so, he said that it should be with understanding as well as in spirit, i.e., with emotional feeling or ecstasy (cf. I Cor. 14:14-17).

Though Paul said he spoke with tongues more than all, he said that he had rather speak only five words in the church with understanding than ten thousand words in a tongue, that by his voice he may edify (cf. vs. 18, 19). Tongues, he continues, when regulated properly in the assembly, signal to unbelievers that the Spirit of God is at work within the church. For only one speaks at a time and an interpreter is present to interpret what is said. But if all speak in tongues at once, unbelievers will conclude the speakers are mad (cf. vs. 22, 23).

Finally, Paul gives a categorical rule of speaking in tongues in verses 27 and 28. He said, *"If any man speak in a tongue, let it be by two, or at the most by three, and that by course; and let one interpret. But if there be no interpreter, let him keep silence in the church; and let him speak to himself, and to God."*

If this regulation of speaking in tongues can so easily be disobeyed by many Pentecostals today, one may justifiably ask, what else in the scriptures can be disobeyed and gotten away with? Yes, Paul did say in verse 39b, *"Forbid not to speak with tongues,"* but that statement by no means contradicted verses 27 and 28, but rather accommodated them.

It should be observed first that the word "unknown" does not appear in the original text of the Bible as it does in I Cor. 14:2, 4, 13, 19, 27. Possibly the translators used the word to distinguish between tongues (plural), *"glossais"* – ethnic dialects or languages – as in Acts 2:4, 6, 8, 11; 10:46 and 19:6 and tongue (singular) *"glosse"* is used when preceded by a singular pronoun which means that a person did not speak in tongues as the disciples did on the Day of Pentecost, but "a" tongue, referring to the Corinthians' *"glossolaly,"* speaking in an unknown utterance. In I Cor. 14:23, preceded by the plural pronoun "all," *"glossais"* is used referring to the Corinthians ecstatic utterances.

Secondly, no interpreter was necessary in either historical account of speaking in tongues for the understanding of the hearers as stated in Acts 2:4, 6, 8, 11. In Corinth, no person at any time should speak in the assembly without an interpreter.

By these two indications, it is hardly possible for one to conclude that the Pentecostal phenomenon and Corinthian phenomenon were identical.

THE DORMANT PERIOD OF TONGUES

~ CHAPTER IV ~
The Dormant Period of Tongues

Although speaking in tongues, as is witnessed today in Pentecostalism, is thought by many to have originated with the Azusa Street Revival in 1906, many scholars of church history inform us that outbreaks of *"glossolalia"* have appeared periodically in the Christian church from the time it appeared in the first century B.C. until the turn of the 19th century. However, only a few sects before then considered tongues as a cardinal doctrine. For that reason, speaking in tongues was never organized into mass denominational form, as is seen today, until about 1910 and on.

One early example of a sect which practiced speaking in tongues appeared about the mid-second century in Phrygia (central Asia Minor) called the Montanists, a charismatic movement led by Montanus and two women, Prisca and Maximila. The Montanists laid much emphasis on special gifts of the Spirit, and claimed that they had "ecstatic experiences, in which they received revelations, saw visions and spoke in ecstatic utterances."[25]

The rise of Montanism was a recurrence "of the emotional element in religion, and a protest against the supremacy of the intellectual factor. It revealed the features of spiritual possession and ecstatic prophecy."[26]

In spite of the good accomplished by this sect, it was short lived because of its ascetic practice and excess legalism.

During the early 17th century there was a Protestant sect called the Camisards living in the southern part of France who protested by force of arms the efforts of Louis XIV to convert them to Catholicism. Their resistance brought about persecution and bloodshed. Their endurance was fortified and their enthusiasm inflamed by Pierre Jurieu, exiled in Rotterdam, whose pastoral letters had much influence on the Protestants

---

[25] Metz, op. cit., p. 26.

[26] George Galloway, *Principles of Religious Development,* MacMillan and Co., Ltd., London, pp. 115-116.

that remained in France. Instead of relinquishing their faith because of the horror of persecution, the Camisards "*. . . fell into frenzy. An infectious ecstasy seized people of all ages and of both sexes. They heard supernatural voices; they spoke with tongues.*"[27] This sect gained a considerable following in both France and England. Their meetings sometimes became so disorderly they had to be restrained by legal force.

"Finally in 1708, they overreached themselves by claiming that one of their number, Thomas Emes, would rise from his grave that year; but the resurrection did not take place, and the resultant disillusionment brought about the speedy decay of the sect."[28]

Some consider the Camisards to be descendents from the Waldensians who revolted against the Roman Catholic Church in the 13th century. The

---

[27] *Encyclopedia of Religion and Ethics,* Charles Scribner's Sons, New York, 1928, Vol. III, p. 176.
[28] Ibid.

phenomenon of *"glossolalia"* has also been reported to have been practiced among the Waldensians.[29]

During the 18th century in America, the Mormons, presently known as the The Church of Jesus Christ of Latter-Day Saints, founded and led by Joseph Smith, Jr., experienced and practiced the phenomenon of speaking in tongues.

In the Book of Mormon, translated from the Plates of Nephi by Joseph Smith, Jr., is found these words. . . "and having the spirit of prophesy, and the spirit of revelation, and also many gifts, the gift of speaking in tongues, and the gift of preaching, and the gift of the Holy Ghost, and the gift of translation. . ." (cf. Alma 9:21, Book of Mormon). Whether Mormonism should be listed as Christian is still debated and possibly will be debated until the return of the Lord. The Mormons believe in and use the Bible as Christians do, but the "Book of Mormon" is considered by the Saints as equal with

---

[29] Vision Synan, *The Holmes Pentecostal Movement in the United States,* Wm. B. Eerdsman Publishing Co., Grand Rapids, MI, 1977, p. 119.

"supporting, but not supplanting" the Bible.[30] Christians or not, they advocate speaking in tongues.

In 1776 the Shakers was founded in North America by Ann Lee (1736-1784) who had joined a sect in England that seceded from the Society of Friends, or the Quakers. Ann Lee professed to be a prophetess and miracle worker. In 1770 she became the spiritual Mother of the sect. In 1774 she came to America and founded the Shaker Society here. The Shakers believed that the sacraments are unnecessary and that all properties should be held in common, as stated in Acts 2:44; 4:32. They were called Shakers because of an ecstatic jerk or body movement seen among them in their services. "The Shakers had also experienced the phenomenon" of *"glossolalia."*[31]

In the early 19th century, Edward Irving (1792-1834), an extremely intelligent and eloquent Presbyterian minister, became pastor of the Caledonian Chapel in London in 1821. In May

---

[30] Frank S. Mead, Samuel S. Hill, rev., *Handbook of Denominations in the United States,* Abingdon Press, Nashville, 1985, p. 134.
[31] Ibid., p. 119.

1827 he became pastor of the National Scotch Church in London. In 1828 Alexander John Scott became Irving's assistant. Scott believed "that the supernatural powers once bestowed upon the church were not merely the phenomenon of one miraculous age, but an inheritance of which she (the church) ought to have possession as surely and richly now as in the days of the Apostles."[32] Edward Irving had already entertained the same idea. In the latter part of 1830 Irving and other evangelical ministers began conducting prayer meetings, "to seek of God the revival of the gifts of the Holy Ghost in the church."[33] In 1831 the gifts of tongues and prophecy appeared among the members of Irving's congregation."[34] However, Irving himself never spoke in tongues. In 1832 the followers of Irving, sometimes called the Irvingites, assumed the title, The Catholic Apostolic Church.

This chapter was designed to point out that speaking in tongues has appeared periodically in the Christian church since the first century and

---

[32] *Encyclopedia of Religion and Ethics,* op. cit., p. 193.
[33] Ibid.
[34] Maurice A. Cannon, *An Encyclopedia of Religion,* Gale Research Company, Detroit, 1970, p. 424.

the much-talked about Azusa Street Revival was only a recurrence of the phenomenon.

THE NEW AWAKENING
OF TONGUES

~ CHAPTER V ~
The New Awakening of Tongues

As has been noted, during the latter part of the 19th century to the first decade of the 20th century, many of the holiness movements fragmented from the older established churches in the United States, mostly from the Baptist and Methodist churches. From those fragmentations many new sects sprang up in many sections of this country; most of them were called holiness movements.

It has also been noted, in the preceding chapter, "The Dormant Period of Tongues," that "glossolalia" appeared periodically in various places and times from the close of the Apostolic Age to the latter period of the 19th century, but was never really considered to be a cardinal doctrine, nor was it ever organized into denominational form as is seen today. Most of the sects seceded from the Catholic Church and because of severe persecution from both church and state, they were either short lived or merged with a larger and more conservative group; e.g., Waldensians of the 13th century merged with the Protestant Reformation.

Although *"glossolalia"* had been witnessed in other revival campaigns before the turn of the century, the Azusa Street revival seems to have played a greater role in the new awakening and widespread practice of the tongues phenomenon than any other revival. Now the Azusa Street revival was by no means extemporaneous. Its beginnings and effect were the result of the preaching and doctrinal concept of Rev. Charles Fox Parham of Topeka, Kansas. Rev. Parham was closely associated with Edward Irving, the founder of the Catholic Apostolic Church. Edward Irving organized, in 1895, the Fire Baptized Holiness Church in Kansas, Oklahoma and Texas. The Fire Baptized Holiness Church was an important link in the formation of modern Pentecostalism. It originated the basic doctrinal premise of the Azusa Revival. In a sense, it was a direct precursor of the Pentecostal movements of today.

Parham, who accepted and espoused the doctrine of a separate baptism of the Holy Ghost apart from sanctification, as interpreted by Irving, opened a school near Topeka, Kansas in 1900. The school remained opened only one year. In the fall of 1905, Parham moved his headquarters to Houston, Texas. In a short time, by the request of friends, he opened The Bible Training School in Houston with an enrollment of about twenty-five students. It was at The Bible Training School that W. J. Seymour, the Azusa Street revivalist, received his theological training.

Seymour, a black Baptist minister, was a native of Louisiana, who early in life moved to Texas. He was an uneducated, poverty-stricken minister. Coming in contact with a holiness movement, he accepted the doctrine of entire sanctification. After hearing of The Bible Training School, Seymour was eager to improve his religious training. But, being a black person, racial customs of the south forbade his entrance. However, seeing his eager desire for knowledge to improve his ministry, Parham permitted him to attend Bible classes during the day. It was under the teaching of Parham that Seymour heard and grasped the new doctrine of Pentecostalism. "He was taught that the holiness movement had been wrong in asserting that sanctification was also the baptism of the Holy Spirit. It was rather a 'third experience' separate in time and nature from the 'second blessing.' Sanctification cleansed and purified the believer, while the baptism with the Holy Spirit brought great power for service."[35]

Parham taught that any other baptism was not the true New Testament baptism unless one had received the "third experience" and spoke in tongues as the 120 disciples did on the day of Pentecost. Whether it was called sanctification or the baptism of fire, it was not enough. In simple language Parham taught that entire sanctification, "the second blessing" taught by John Wesley, is not the baptism of the New Testament. But there must be a "third experience," the result of "the baptism," as he called it.

Some Pentecostals are still divided on this issue as to whether the "second blessing" or the "third experience" is the result of the baptism of the Holy Ghost.

---

[35] Vision Synan, op. cit., 103-104.

Seymour accepted the teachings of Parham without question or criticism. However, he did not speak in tongues or receive the "third experience" until he was invited to Los Angeles by Miss Neely Terry, whom he met while in school at Houston, Texas. Miss Terry recommended Seymour to be pastor at a small Black Nazarene Holiness Church whose members had been driven from Second Baptist Church for embracing the doctrine of holiness.

The Nazarene mission had elected a Mrs. Hutchinson as acting pastor. When Miss Terry recommended that Seymour come to assume the duties as pastor, he was accepted. He arrived in Los Angeles in early April, 1906, not realizing that he was on a mission that would earn for him the title, "Father of Modern Pentecostalism."

Seymour preached his first sermon from Acts 2:4 and declared that the only Bible evidence of having received the "third experience" was speaking in tongues. Yet, he still had not experienced *"glossolalia."* Mrs. Hutchinson, feeling that his teaching was contrary to the accepted holiness views of the church, forbade him to preach the next night. Many of the members accepted his message with enthusiasm.

Seymour then began preaching in the living room of Mr. Richard Asbury at 216 Bonnie Brae Street. While in a series of prayer meetings on April 9, 1906, Seymour and several others fell to the floor and began to speak in tongues. In the following services, the demonstration of tongues was so pronounced that many people came to see what this mystery was all about.

After the crowd became too large and noisy, it was necessary for Seymour to find another place to hold his meetings. He soon found an old abandoned Methodist building at 312 Azusa Street to continue his services. Soon after Seymour started preaching in the building at Azusa Street, a revival began in which "scores of people began to fall under the Power, and arise speaking in other tongues."[36]

---

[36] Ibid., p. 107.

THE PENTECOSTAL HERITAGE LANDMARK

Current Museum
The Beginnings of Modern Pentecostalism

216 N. Bonnie Brae
Los Angeles, California

As the revival continued, news spread throughout the United States. People came to Los Angeles by train loads every day. Some were curious and some serious. They witnessed people, men and women, white and black, being so overcome during the service that they "would shout, weep, dance, fall into trances, speak and sing in tongues, and interpret the message in English."[37]

By the summer of 1906 people from all over the country were arriving and attending the revival, and complete integration prevailed in all meetings. "Blacks, whites, Chinese and even Jews attended side by side to hear Seymour preach."[38]

But not everyone who attended the Azusa Mission accepted its proceedings. Some were critical of the extreme emotionalism and enthusiasm that characterized the meetings. It was also noticeable that spiritualists and mediums from the various cults of the city were in attendance practicing their séances, trances and hypnosis.

---

[37] Ibid., p. 108.
[38] Ibid., p. 109.

Seymour wrote to his teacher, Parham, for advice as to how to handle the evil, and invited him to come to Los Angeles to supervise the revival. Before Parham's arrival, someone reported to him that Seymour's meetings were becoming more and more like the old camp meetings among colored folks and that white people were imitating the crude unintelligent Negroes of the south. Although Seymour attempted to de-emphasize tongues to control the zealous crowds, his efforts were not accepted. Another visitor to the mission reported that people were singing songs in a far-away tune that sounded unnatural and repulsive, and that there was kissing between sexes and even races.

Parham arrived in Los Angeles in October, 1906. Upon his coming to the Azusa Street Mission, he was astounded at the "holy roller" aspect of the services and at the spiritualists and hypnotists who, by this time, seemed to have taken over the Mission. Parham attempted to correct the fanaticism which had, in his opinion, gone beyond the limits of common sense and reason. He denounced the hypnotists and spiritualists.

Parham was told after preaching a few times by one of Seymour's members that he was not wanted in the Azusa Mission. Parham left the Mission and opened services in a building on the corner of Broadway and Temple Street. This meeting was short-lived.

Soon after Parham was denied privilege to preach in the Azusa Street Mission, a breach between Seymour and his father in the gospel occurred which was never overcome. Later, Parham denounced Seymour and the Azusa Street meetings as mere fits and spasms, like the "holy rollers and hypnotists" meetings. However, this breach did not deter the Azusa Street Revival.

Though many came to the revival for different reasons, most of them accepted the teaching and preaching of Seymour and returned to their churches endeavoring to promulgate the same to their members.

Not only did this revival affect this country, but also Europe, Norway, Canada and even India, where meetings were held with all the characteristics of the Azusa Street Revival.

Rev. T. B. Barrat, a Methodist pastor of Oslo, Norway, who came to New York on a tour, began to correspond with Seymour about the Pentecostal doctrine. While in New York, Barrat received the Pentecostal experience. Upon returning home, Barrat soon had both Methodists and Baptists speaking in tongues. "He was credited with starting Pentecostal movements in Sweden, Norway, Denmark, Germany, France and England."[39]

However, in spite of the later rift that came between Seymour and Parham, student and teacher; in spite of the fact that "Parham spent the later years of his life as an avid supporter of the Klu Klux Klan;"[40] and in spite of *"glossolalia,"* having been experienced in various places at various times in the Christian church before 1906, the Azusa Street Revival, headed by a black, crude uneducated preacher, became the catalyst, either directly or indirectly, for the formation of most, if not all, Pentecostal denominations since 1906. Practically all

---

[39] Ibid., p. 114.
[40] Ibid., p. 108.

Pentecostals can trace their roots to the Azusa Street Revival.

The Azusa Street Mission was demolished in 1928 soon after Seymour's death. Parham returned to his home in Baxter Springs, Kansas where he died in 1929. Yet their revivals in Los Angeles and Topeka were destined to write a most important chapter in the history of Christianity.

FALL-OUT OF MODERN PENTECOSTALISM

~ CHAPTER VI ~
The Fall-Out of Modern Pentecostalism

From the time of the mid-second century until the New Awakening of the 20th century, *"glossolalia"* was unacceptable in public worship by the Catholic and the mainline Protestant churches. It was looked upon as religious fanaticism mainly for the poor and unlearned. Some judged it as the work of the devil. It was an issue that brought about much misunderstanding and persecution upon those who practiced it. For this reason, many sects were short-lived and faded from existence.

After the Reformation, the pressure was somewhat abated, and, as time went on, those speaking in tongues were not so severely persecuted or abused. However, they continued to be viewed with much disfavor and contempt.

As mentioned in the previous chapter, the Azusa Street Revival of 1906 opened the doors of Pentecostalism throughout the world. Further, speaking in tongues became a cardinal doctrine of Pentecostalism and this inevitably resulted in the formation of denominational organizations. Today, amongst the many organized denominations that sprang up from the Azusa Street Revival, there is an aggregate membership of approximately 12 million.

Today, many of the mainline churches which frowned on *"glossolalia"* are not only favoring it, but encouraging their members to seek the experience – seek the baptism of the Holy Ghost evidenced by *"glossolalia."*

The Charismatic Renewal Movement has done much to bridge the chasm between Pentecostalism and the mainline churches, and, the Renewal Movement can, in like manner, trace its lineage to Azusa Street Revival.

The Charismatic Movement is not a religious denomination but it is comprised of members of many Christian denominations.

The Charismatic Movement had its beginning in 1958. It is credited to a group in an Episcopal Church in Van Nuys, California, and was thusly called Charismatic Movement to be distinguished from the already established Pentecostal churches. The Movement was not designed to bring about the division in the mainline churches nor to be organized into a denomination but rather to replace the monotony and emptiness of the old ritualistic and institutionalized forms of worship. To accomplish this aim, they proposed to awaken in the church a need for the exercise of the spiritual gifts of the early church as cited by St. Paul in Rom. 12:6-6; I Cor. 12:7-10, 28; Eph. 4:11. Their claims quickly penetrated every major denomination across America and continue to spread throughout the perimeters of the Christian world. Even American Catholics, including some priests and nuns, were soon taken by the "fall out" of this "new penetration."

The rapidly spreading enthusiasm of the Charismatic Movement has made great strides in affecting the ecumenical practice across denominational lines. In many cities across America, the clergy of most denominations --

Protestant, Pentecostal and Catholic -- are meeting and praying together and forming interdenominational committees, discussing religious, economic, political and social issues for the betterment of the community or city as a whole.

Nevertheless, the Charismatic Movement mirrored an informal and secular image much like that of the time and passion of its emergence. It was anti-institutional and anti-ecclesiastical. Instead of conventional actions, it gave opportunity for personal freedom of expression and individualism. The Charismatics believed that if the Holy Ghost speaks through any person at any time, the need for the clergy or any ecclesiastical authority would be lessened.

In their beginning most charismatic groups preferred meeting in unstructured and informal settings rather than in the church, where worshippers were expected to conform to some conventional norm. But their method of worship "was superseded by the demands of the 1960s and 1970s that people should "do their own thing," and "let it all hang out," as the colloquial slogans of the time suggested. The clergy, as authority figures, were in part the butt of these trends."[41]

The movement succeeded in giving opportunity for more lay participation in worship services. And inasmuch as it had no organizational structure, "It represented a movement within the churches rather than a division from them."[42]

If the Pentecostal movements counted all those affected by the fallout of the *"glossolalia"* phenomenon, their memberships well exceed 15 million. This number includes some who are sanctified and have never spoken in tongues, and some who speak in tongues who have never been saved, and some who have backslidden and are still speaking in tongues. As in other denominations, there are some who are sanctified yet say very little; there are others who "shout" and "praise" who have never been saved and still others who have backslidden and can still speak the holiness language very fluently.

---

[41] John McManners, *The Oxford Illustrated History of Christianity,* Oxford University Press, Oxford, 1990, p. 589.
[42] Ibid., p. 585.

MUST ALL SPEAK IN TONGUES?

~ CHAPTER VII ~
Must All Speak in Tongues?

True, there are many passages of scripture that may require some theological training or some logical reasoning to interpret their meanings, but the subject of this chapter as it pertains to St. Paul's question asked to the Corinthians in I Cor. 12:30b needs no scholarly interpretation to conclude that the answer is a categorical **"No."**

Paul declares that if all members of the body were one member, and that member played one role in the body, there would be no body (cf. I Cor. 12:19, 20, 27-30b). These verses of scripture should adequately convince those who have not experienced the phenomenon that speaking in tongues is not a mandatory experience for all saints any more than any other gift of the Spirit.

It would be understandable if any other passage of scripture could be found in the Bible that gives the slightest implication that the verses above may be interpreted to mean that all should speak in tongues.

If the baptism or filling of the Holy Ghost manifests itself in the form of a gift to prove its presence and power, tongues – one of the least of all spiritual gifts and the gift most likely to be imitated by non-spiritual influences – would very likely not be the gift.

Love is the most unmistakable identity by which the Holy Ghost manifests Himself. This is consistently demonstrated throughout scripture, and thusly, forms the basis for all Christian faith.

Conclusion

The issue of *"glossolalia,"* speaking in tongues, is one of complexity. And there are no categorical statements in scripture to which one may appeal that can be considered the end of all arguments. This being the case, whether one argues *"glossolalia,"* pro or con, one's argument does not rest on a clear statement of scripture but rather on a series of reasonable deductions.

The writer has used this method of argument, not as an attack on saints who speak in tongues, but as a defense for saints who do not speak in tongues.

First, the writer has already endeavored to establish the fact that "the tongues" (plural) -- intelligible languages spoken on the day of Pentecost (Acts 2:4), at Cornelius' house (Acts 10:46), and in Ephesus (Acts 19:6) -- were not identical to a "tongue" (singular), ecstatic or charismatic utterance spoken by the Corinthians.

The one was a direct enduement of the Holy Ghost with power. The other, without doubt, was influenced primarily by emotional ecstasy with praise.

Second, measure, if you will, the priority and popularity granted speaking in tongues by the Corinthians, the Pentecostals and other charismatic movements by that of the New Testament, and observe how speaking in tongues loses its luster in the glow of many other gifts, whether spiritual or natural, more useful and effective than tongues.

Third, it must be remembered that speaking in tongues is a familiar practice of Hinduism, Islam, Mormonism and Spiritualism. That being true, one should view with keen reservation any doctrine that claims that speaking in tongues is the only evidence of the baptism of the Holy Ghost. Therefore, it is evident that speaking in tongues can be induced either by the spirit of error or the Spirit of Truth. One writer claims that "in nearly all religions at the point where fervor merges into fanaticism there are similar manifestations."[43] Whether that religion is orthodox, heterodox or anti-Christian, the manifestations are similar. Emotional feeling can be, and has too often been, mistaken for spiritual fervor. It is, "...a perilous guide, and cannot be trusted to lead those who follow it to the land of light."[44]

This does not imply that feeling plays no part in religion. Religion is more dependent upon feeling than it is on dry intellect. No religion can ever flourish apart from an atmosphere of feeling. Yet emotional feelings can easily disengage the mind and will be manifested in fast and oft repeated clichés like, "Let everybody say 'amen,' or 'hallelujah,' or 'praise the Lord,' or 'clap your hands'." Or, there may be songs that repeat one word over and over again. This can often result in the suspension of the sense of reason and the manifestation of some kind of ecstatic action,

---

[43] Sanders, J. Oswald. Spiritual Maturity: Principles of Spiritual Growth for Every Believer. (Moody Bible Institute of Chicago, 1962, 1964) p. 203.

[44] Galloway, George. The Principles of Religious Development: A Psychological and Philosophical Study. (University of California Libraries, 1909) p. 101.

e.g., speaking in tongues, violent shouting, fainting or dancing. But seldom do any of these things take place when prayers, songs, testimonies and words of edification engage the mind, the will and the emotion.

Fourth, from Romans to Jude, there are twenty-one epistles: fourteen Pauline epistles and seven general epistles, comprising one hundred twenty-one chapters. Only three chapters of one of those letters refer to speaking in tongues; i.e., I Cor. 12 – 14, and at no time in those three chapters does the writer, St. Paul, promote tongues.

Peter, while writing to all the churches in Asia Minor, addressed them as "elect...through sanctification of the Spirit" (I Peter 1:2); yet, nowhere does he refer to tongues. Neither does John, writing to all Christian churches, ever mention tongues in his three epistles.

Therefore, it is clearly seen that speaking in tongues is not so prioritized in the 21 epistles, or anywhere else in the New Testament. Would it not be wise for one to prayerfully and carefully re-examine the much exaggerated and unscriptural claims of tongues before seeking that particular gift?

Regarding tongues, C. P. Jones, founder of the Church of Christ (Holiness) U.S.A., took the following position:

1. That no one gift is the specific sign or evidence of the Holy Spirit's presence, but faith (Heb. 11) and love (I Cor. 13:13) are the evidences; not even power alone is the evidence for that may be of Satan.

2. That these gifts, though they may be of use to edification, may be counterfeited and are not to be trusted as evidence (II Thess. 2: 7-12; II Tim. 3:8)

3. That there are three essential evidences of true religion. They are Faith, Hope and Love. (I Cor. 13:13).

4. That the Bible endorses speaking in tongues, or a gift of tongues, but that no one really speaks in tongues unless he speaks a language understood by men, as in Acts 2 [vv. 4, 6, 8].

5. That though one speaks [in] tongues, it is no evidence of the Holy Ghost at all, but merely a sign.[45]

As stated in number four of the quote from C. P. Jones, "That the Bible endorses speaking in tongues. . .but no one really speaks in tongues unless he speaks a language understood by men" (Acts 2:4, 6, 8). Paul refers to tongues as a Spiritual gift in I Corinthians 12:10b as *"hetero,"* different kinds of tongues as spoken on the Day of Pentecost and not an unknown tongue as spoken in the Corinthian church.

It is clearly seen that speaking in unknown tongues adds nothing whatsoever to the spirituality, the maturity and the moral conduct of those who have experienced it. It is enough in itself to help one realize that the claims given it today are terribly and unscripturally exaggerated (cf. I Cor. 3:1, 2; 5:1).

However, Pentecostalism is not pagan, occultic, heterodox nor hypocritical, although some of its

---

[45] Manual, Church of Christ (Holiness) U.S.A., Rev. Ed. (Third), 1968; pp. 25, 26.

followers are, as in all other denominations, hypocritical. Pentecostalism is made up of sincere, Bible-believing evangelical preachers and laymen. Many of them are highly educated and refined as is in any other denomination.

What do the Pentecostals have that the non-Pentecostals do not have? The answer is nothing spiritual. It is not what they have or do not have that makes the difference. The difference lies in their commitment to what they are doing and the degree of vitality and zeal with which they use what they have. Non-Pentecostals can learn much from that.

The author realizes that this book, as in other writing, has not succeeded in resolving the issue of *"glossolalia"* in the Christian church, but the following words of the wise man, Solomon, may give some consolation. *"And further, by these, my son, be admonished: of the making of many books there is no end; and much study is a weariness of the flesh. Let us hear the conclusion of the whole matter: Fear God and keep his commandments: for this is the whole duty of man. For God shall bring every work into judgment, with every secret thing, whether it be good, or whether it be evil"* (Eccles.12:12-14).

Must one speak or not speak? Conclusively, to speak is none better; to not speak is none the worse – *in tongues, that is.*

About the Author

O. W. McInnis began his ministry in 1939. He pastored congregations in Kansas, Virginia, Illinois and Indiana. He was the editor of the H.Y.P.U. training manual, *The Compass,* during the early part of his ministry. He served as an instructor and writer for the Chicago Christian Education Conference sponsored by The Urban Ministry for a number of years. He also lectured at seminars and workshops for various religious denominations. Among his colleagues he was affectionately known as "The Dean of Preachers." Bishop McInnis served as a presiding bishop in the Church of Christ (Holiness) USA from 1956 until his retirement in 1990.

Following his retirement and, after much prayer and guidance from the Lord, Bishop McInnis explored the issue of "speaking in tongues as evidence of the Holy Spirit in one's spiritual walk with God" in a book entitled, *"To Speak or Not to Speak - In Tongues, That Is."*

The bishop and his wife of 65 years resided in Virginia Beach, VA until they went home to be with the Lord; she, in September, 1999; he, in June, 2004.

His heart's desire was to hear our Lord say, *"Well done, thou good and faithful servant."*

The O.W. and Mae Julia McInnis School of Ministries and Christian Education has been established at Gospel Mission Temple, Davenport, Iowa in their honor, where Bishop Jimmie R. Horton is the pastor.